# Hawai'i Volcanoes National Park Coloring Book

By KEITH L. HOOFNAGLE

HAWAI'I NATURAL HISTORY ASSOCIATION



ISBN 0-940295-07-5

Kīlauea Visitor Center

A Park Ranger or Hawai'i Natural History Association employee will welcome you to Hawai'i Volcanoes National Park. He or she will be happy to answer your questions.

There are interesting exhibits to see in the Kīlauea (<u>KEY</u>-LAH-WAY-AH) Visitor Center. A free volcano movie is shown in the auditorium.

The old Volcano House was built as a hotel in 1877. It is the oldest hotel still standing in the state of Hawai'i.

The building has been carefully restored by the National Park Service. It now houses the Volcano Art Center Gallery, where local artisans display and sell works inspired by the volcano area. It is next door to the Kīlauea Visitor Center.

Across the street, a modern Volcano House stands on the rim of Kīlauea Caldera. It features a hotel and restaurant with a fine view of the caldera.

When an eruption occurs the guests are notified by the staff — so no one misses the show!

EARTHQUAKE
TRAIL

Hiking is fun at Hawai'i Volcanoes. A variety of trails offers something for everyone.

An easy half-hour walk will take you from the Volcano House down the Earthquake Trail to Waldron Ledge and back again. Other trails can lead you across Kīlauea Caldera or many miles into the park back-country for overnight camping.

Ask for trail information at the visitor center and always be sure that you are prepared for the hike you plan to take.

Sometimes, when Kīlauea erupts, it throws tiny bits of rock, called ash, into the air. The ash may be blown for miles on the wind before it falls to the ground. Long ago, people walked on this soft volcanic ash in the Ka'ū Desert. The ash hardened and their footprints were preserved in the "mud."

Steam coming from vents in the ground along the Crater Rim Drive shows us that there is enough volcanic heat under the ground to turn rainwater into steam. The steam is hot and the cracks are deep. Stay on marked trails and don't get too close.

Kīlauea Military Camp is the only active military camp within a National Park. It provides rest and recreation for men and women from all branches of the United States Armed Forces.

KOA'E KEA
(White-Tailed Tropicbird)

Two birds you might see in the park are the Koa'e Kea (KO-AH-EH KAY-AH), seen flying above the craters where it nests, and the Kōlea (<u>KO</u>-LAY-AH), common on lawns where it feeds.

KŌLEA
(Pacific Golden Plover)

Scientists at the Hawaiian Volcano Observatory learn about the volcanoes by studying them close up.

Seismographs record earthquakes and tell us how big they are. Sometimes they even tell the scientists when a volcano will erupt.

At the Jaggar Museum you can learn about how volcanoes work and see seismographs in action.

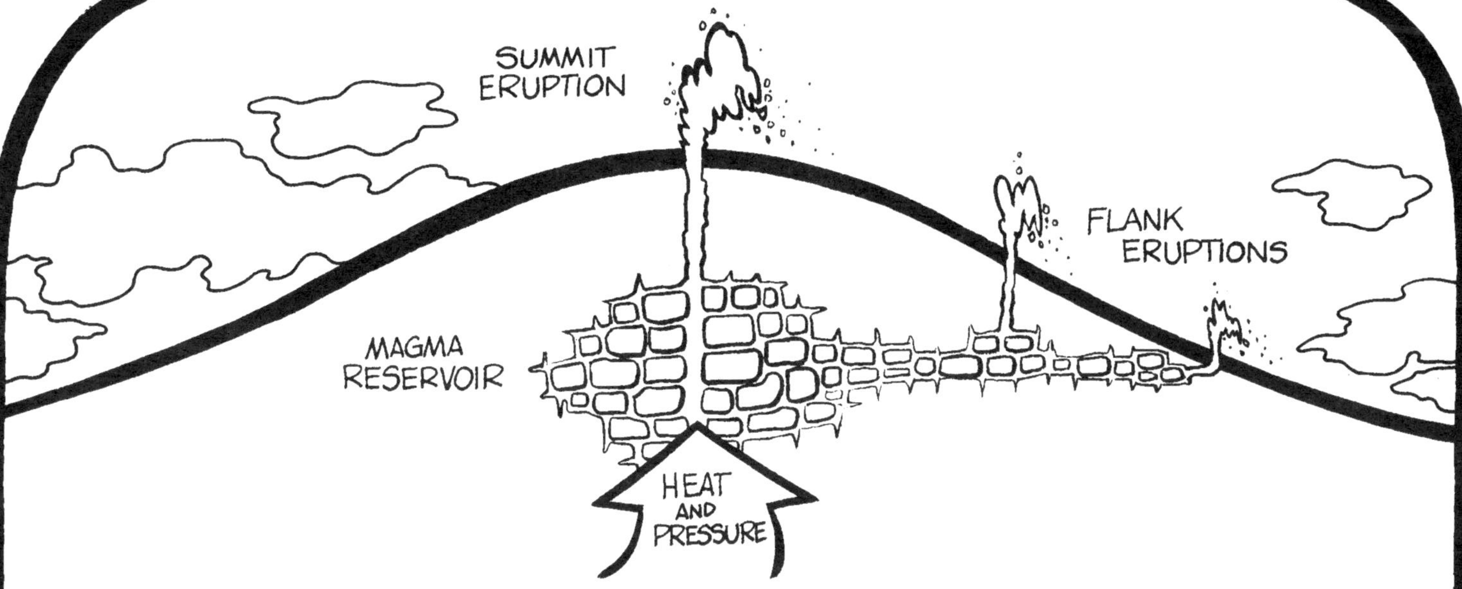


Volcanoes in Hawai'i are called SHIELD volcanoes because of their shape. They are formed by many layers of very hot, runny lava which comes through cracks in the earth's crust. They seldom explode, but sometimes they send lava fountains hundreds of feet into the air.

The native Hawaiians recognized two different kinds of lava. They called the smooth kind pāhoehoe (<u>PA</u>-HOY-HOY) and the chunky kind 'a'ā (AH-<u>AH</u>). Scientists borrowed the names and today they are used by people everywhere. Be sure to look for these lavas in the park.

PĀHOEHOE

'A'Ā

The Crater Rim Drive circles the summit caldera of Kīlauea. A short walk from a parking area will take you to Halema‘uma‘u (HA-LAY-MA-OO-MA-OO) Crater. This crater is historically the most active vent of Kīlauea volcano. It has been an overflowing lava lake and now it is a deep steaming pit.

From Halema‘uma‘u you can see the summit of Mauna Loa (MAO-NAH LOW-AH), considered the largest volcano on earth. Both Kīlauea and Mauna Loa are still growing and changing. If you see an eruption you'll know this is true.

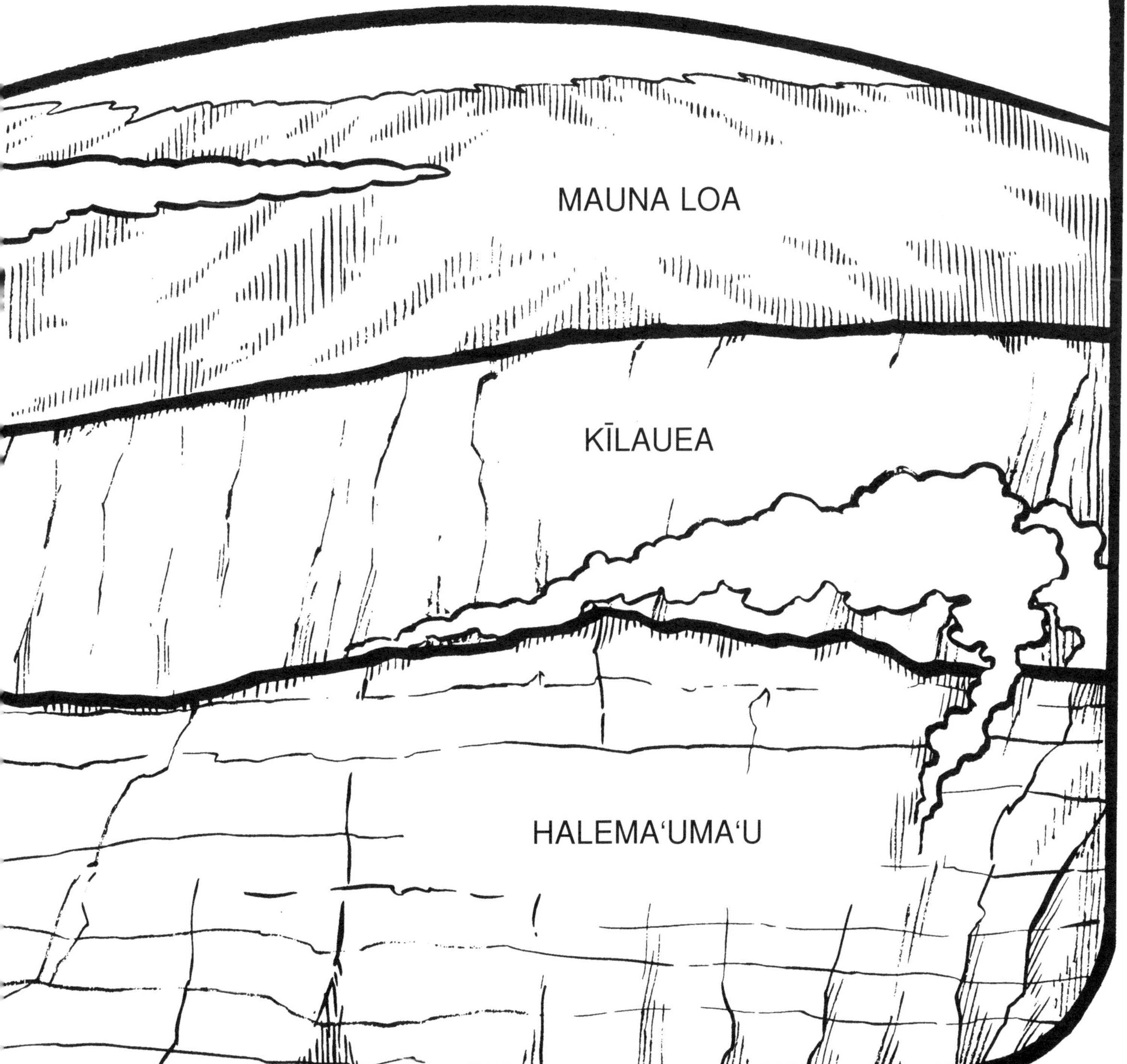

Kīlauea Iki (KEY-LAH-WAY-AH EE-KEY) erupted in 1959 destroying a forest with hot cinders and creating the interesting landscape you will see along the Devastation Trail.

Thurston Lava Tube, Nāhuku (<u>NAH</u>-HOO-KOO), was formed when a lava flow cooled and hardened on the surface but kept on flowing underneath. The cave-like tube was left when the fluid center drained out.

KĪLAUEA IKI

CHAIN OF CRATERS ROAD

A scenic road leaves the Crater Rim Drive near Kīlauea Iki. It follows a "chain of craters" which extends along a fault from the summit of Kīlauea. This road leads to unusual volcanic formations created by Mauna Ulu (MAO-NAH OO-LOO), and sweeping ocean views. The road ends in the park's coastal area where it has been covered by lava many times since 1986.

Rock walls and other ruins are all that remain of Hawaiian villages once found in the coastal area of the park.

A typical homestead or kuleana (KOO-LAY-AH-NAH) may have provided a place for a garden and separate hale (HAH-LAY) for sleeping and cooking.

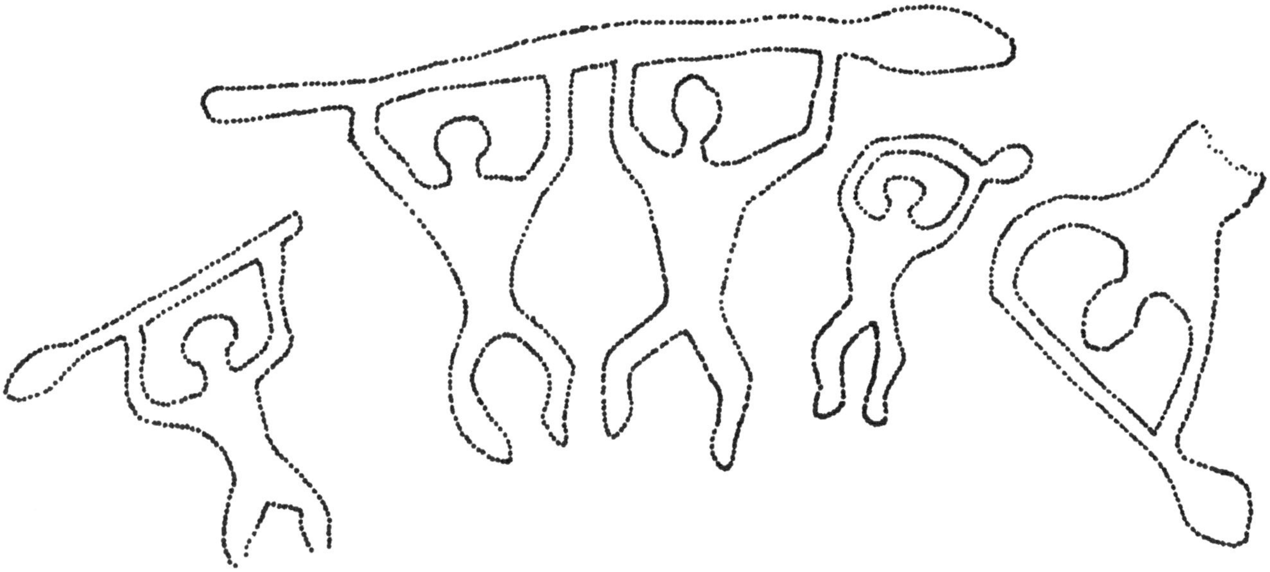

Petroglyphs (rock carvings) tell us stories about Hawaiian activities of the past.

Please help protect these one-of-a-kind pictures by watching where you step.

The nēnē (NAY-NAY) or Hawaiian goose was nearly extinct in 1940.

People from all over the world helped to save it. Nēnē are now being carefully raised and released back into the wild.

You can help protect the state bird of Hawai‘i. Do not feed nēnē. Feeding attracts the nēnē to parking areas and roadsides where they can be hit by cars.

Some birds are found only in Hawai‘i. Native Hawaiian birds you might see at Hawai‘i Volcanoes National Park:

ʻŌʻŌ

But you'll never see the black and yellow ʻŌʻō (OH-OH) except in pictures. Common on the island of Hawaiʻi many years ago, it is now extinct. That means gone forever.

COMMON MYNAH

Introduced birds, such as the brown-colored Mynah from India, compete with native birds and sometimes bring them diseases. More native birds will disappear unless people work together to save them.

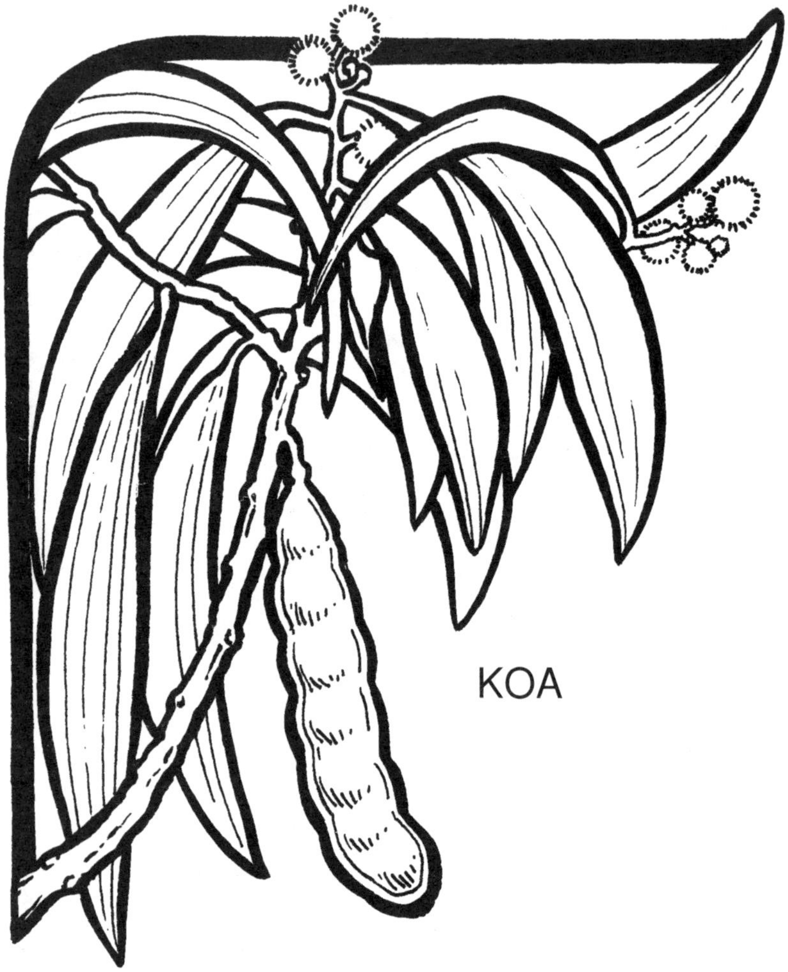

KOA

ʻŌHIʻA LEHUA

HĀPUʻU
(Tree Fern)

Native Hawaiian plants are special because many of them are found nowhere else in the world. They need places like National Parks to protect them.

Three native plants you might see are the Koa (KO-AH) with curved leaves, the red-flowered ʻŌhiʻa Lehua (O-HEE-AH LAY-WHO-AH), and the bright green Hāpuʻu (HA-POO-OO).

Most of the plants Hawai'i is known for were brought to the islands by people.

Three introduced plants you might see are on this page. Ginger blossoms are yellow or white. Tritonia flowers are bright orange, and orchids are purple.

Introduced plants are not always good for native plants. They may be one of the reasons that native plants are getting scarce.

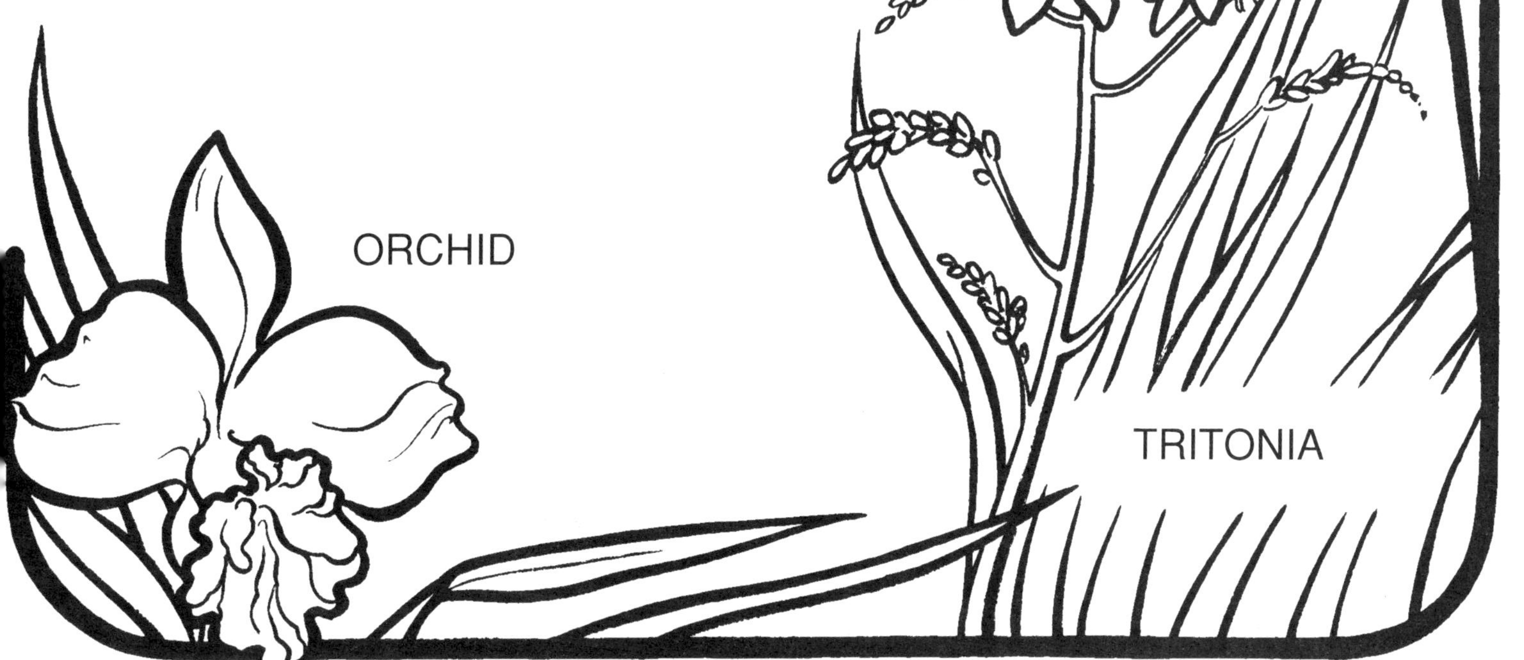

The native plants and animals of Hawai'i are fragile and their natural balance is easily upset.

Biologists in the park are trying to control introduced animals such as the goat, mongoose, and pig, so native species can survive.

With the care of the park staff and visitors, Hawai'i Volcanoes National Park can continue to protect Hawaiian cultural sites, geological formations, and native plants and animals.

MONGOOSE
PIG

# BE VERY CAREFUL

## IN HAWAI'I VOLCANOES NATIONAL PARK

➢ STAY ON THE TRAIL

Deep cracks, steaming vents and steep cliffs make hiking off trails dangerous.

➢ WATCH YOUR STEP

Lava rock is crumbly and it's easy to lose your footing. Lava rock is sharp and can cut.

➢ STAY AWAY FROM VOLCANIC FUMES

Breathing sulfur fumes can make you feel sick.